THE *Beloved* CALLS

Workbook

Written by Jessica Zeibig

THE BELOVED CALLS

Jessica Zeibig 2023

First published by Daniel Hagen Ministries 2023

www.danielhagenministries.com

All rights reserved. Without limiting the rights under copyright reserved above, no part of this publication may be reproduced, stored in or introduced into a database and retrieval system or transmitted in any form or any means (electronic, mechanical, photocopying, recording or otherwise) without the prior written permission of both the owner of the copyright and the above publishers. The only exception is brief quotations in printed reviews.

Printed by IngramSpark
ISBN: 978-0-6454722-8-8
ISBN Ebook: 978-0-6454722-9-5

Unless otherwise specified, all scripture taken from the New King James Version, Copyright 1982 by Thomas Nelson. Used by permission. All rights reserved.

Cover design by Jessica Zeibig

ACKNOWLEDGMENTS

Daniel Hagen, you have supported and encouraged me to write this workbook for Revival Ready School, and I value so highly your investment and trust in me. I really honour you and Chelsea as pastors, leaders and friends. I am so grateful for the way you have championed me and propelled me within a safe space into pursuing the call of God on my life. I honour both yourself and Chelsea for your character, integrity and Christ-like hearts. Thank you.

Anton and Bev Bekker, thank you for your investment into reviewing, editing and organising the publishing of this book. I value your time, your input, your encouragement, and your humour! Thank you for the laughs.

Peter and Suzie Botross, thank you for everything that you poured into me over the years. You have played a truly instrumental part in my journey, and I am eternally grateful for your love, your time, your wisdom, your challenging, your teaching, your sharpening, your encouragement, your support and your prayers. You guys are pure gold.

My family; Mum, Dad, Vlad, Grandma, Grandpa, Alisha, Ryan, Daniel, Elle and Sophie Van Den Acker, yes Sophie, I place you with my family, Achoti! I love you all so much and am so thankful for you always pushing me closer to Jesus, for loving me unconditionally, and for encouraging me to do the hard things, and do them well! Thank you for every prayer, every tear, every hug and every inspiring word. Thank you for your roles in shaping me into who I am today, walking in the fullness of who God created me to be.

Ella and Leo, my two beautiful children. Watching you both blossom in your own relationships with Jesus has been a beautiful journey that has taught me so much. Thank you for the time you have both given me to write, and for being my greatest supporters and cheer squad! You two are my biggest blessings, and I couldn't be prouder of the amazing little Jesus-lovers you both are. Thank you for making me smile and laugh every single day. Writing this wouldn't have been the same without learning from you. I love you both to the moon and back 100 million times!!

And last, but certainly not least, Jesus. My best friend. The time spent at your feet as I wrote, soaking in your presence, has truly marked me. You supernaturally gave me the endurance to pump this out in a short time, and led me so beautifully into the secret place to write, no matter where I was writing from! I love you with everything, You have my whole heart and forever my 'yes'. You transformed my life, making beauty from ashes. This is for you, and I pray it brings you honour and helps lead your church closer to you.

CONTENTS

Introduction ...pg 1

THE SECRET PLACE ...pg 2
- An Invitation
- Surrender

DWELLING AND ABIDING ...pg 12
- Abiding in His Shadow
- Waiting on the Lord
- Seeking

HOME OF THE HOLY SPIRIT ...pg 23
- It's what's Inside that Counts

LIVING IN PURITY ...pg 33
- Keeping our Eyes, Ears & Minds Pure
- Living as Children of Light

THE OIL OF INTIMACY ...pg 41
- The Oil.
- Keeping the Lamp Burning
- Tunnel Vision

CONTENTS

LOVING ...pg 52
- Loving Well
- Love and Unity

WORSHIP AND PRAYER ...pg 60
- Daily Worship
- Coming before God
- Prayer
- Praying in the Holy Spirit
- Positioning Yourself Physically
- Worship
- Fasting

NAMES OF GOD ...pg 73

REPENTANCE AS A LIFESYLE ...pg 81
- What is Repentance?

GLORY HOST ...pg 88

INTRODUCTION

Who will sacrifice their own life and keep their lamps burning continuously for the Beloved? Who will pursue the call to intimacy, purity and holiness? Who will go deep in surrender and sit at His feet? Who will walk in obedience and live a life of pure devotion?

Revival is exciting, and to see all that God is doing across the nations is amazing. However, it's so easy to get excited and caught up in what He does, forgetting who He is. We need to realise that true revival starts on the inside of us through a relationship with God which then overflows out of us, reviving the nations. A word God gave me in June 2023 was "inside out revival". This revival needs to start on the inside of us as followers of Christ Jesus, then work its way out to impact the world!

Revival in my own life began back in 2017. I had come back to Christ after years of emptiness and turmoil, which was followed by years of wishy-washy, lukewarm Christianity. I was so confused about not seeing today what I would read about in my Bible, and so I would question God and question the authenticity of the body of Christ.
Then one Sunday morning at the back of my Baptist church, everything changed. I was a tired, single mum with her baby, only months old, in her arms, starving for more. In one single moment of wholehearted surrender God showed up and proved himself in a profound way and I experienced for myself His true power and love, which transformed every sphere of my life. This lead to a deep hunger and thirst in me for more of the true and living God!

By cultivating a lifestyle of devotion, pursuing holiness and walking in faith, a revival took place inside me and a beautiful relationship with God was birthed.

These are some of the things I have learnt along the way.

THE SECRET PLACE

An invitation

Revelation 3:20, **"Behold, I stand at the door and knock. If anyone hears My voice and opens the door, I will come in to him and dine with him, and he with Me."**
We have been given a personal invitation to enter into a secret place to dine with Christ. This is usually done in private and is a place, spiritually, where we can know and experience His glorious presence. It is a place of surrender, where you can let go and empty yourself, allowing the oil of His Spirit to fill you.

Taking time out to be with God is following an example that Jesus gives us throughout scripture. It was vital to His ministry and is vital to ours. Being firmly planted with strong roots in Him (which grow and strengthen in the secret place) produces fruit and allows us to prosper.
Psalm 1:2-3, **"But his delight is in the law of the LORD, And in His law he meditates day and night. He shall be like a tree, planted by the rivers of water, that brings forth its fruit in its season, whose leaf also shall not wither; and whatever he does shall prosper."**
The word 'prosper' here in Hebrew means *'tsaw-lakh'* which means; to push forward, break out, come (mightily), go over, be good, be meet, be profitable, prosperity, prosperous, prosperously.

To be prosperous and produce good fruit, we must accept the invitation to draw near to Him.

It also allows us to be pruned by Him, which is super important in our growth!
In this secret place our relationship with Christ develops and grows, drawing us into deeper intimacy with Him making us more effective for His Kingdom. Familiarity doesn't usher in the presence of God, INTIMACY does. His Spirit is IN us, but it's up to us to partner with Him in the secret place to make His presence real and tangible.

The term "secret place" in Hebrew is *cether/satar* which means "to hide or be concealed." This word is used in Psalm 91 and Psalm 32:7.

Psalm 32:7 reads, **"You are my hiding place; you will protect me from trouble and surround me with songs of deliverance."**
The secret place can refer to a physical location, but usually refers to our heart or a spiritual state in relationship with God, being supernaturally "hidden" in His Spirit (as described in the Hebrew root word)

Psalm 91:1 reads, **"He who dwells in the secret place of the Most High shall abide under the shadow of the Almighty".**
Dwelling in the secret place of the Most High and abiding in His shadow are key aspects of the secret place. When we come before Christ to dwell in the secret place, we are leaving the cares and concerns of the day and quieting our hearts before Him.

James 4:8 says, **"Draw near to God and He will draw near to you".**
It's our choice to receive the invitation and GO THERE, to draw near, into the secret place with Him.

Surrender

Complete surrender to the Holy Spirit helps us get to the secret place with Him.
I love the phrase "outwards actions for inward reactions".

Psalm 1:2-3 reads **"But his delight is in the law of the LORD, And in His law he meditates day and night. He shall be like a tree planted by the rivers of water, that brings forth its fruit in its season, whose leaf also shall not wither; And whatever he does shall prosper."**

Delighting, meditating, being like a tree planted by the rivers of water (rivers of water often represents the Holy Spirit in the Bible), having strong roots and a firm foundation in Christ are keys to unlocking a deeper relationship with Him. And being PLANTED there, in that heart space, brings fruit & whatever you do will prosper - it's the outward action of surrender and the inward reaction of your Spirit coming into alignment with His Holy Spirit.

Being in the place of surrender means spending time at His feet and giving everything to Jesus in secret and letting Him come and fill you up. As you empty your heart and soul of everything, you make room for Him to fill you.

2 Kings 4:3-4 is a great illustration of being an empty vessel which enables you to carry the oil He wants to pour out on you. This is important; you've got to be IN the glory (in the manifest presence and power of God that comes through relationship with Him), to CARRY the glory.

We often see in scripture that the effectiveness of people in ministry was a direct result of their relationship with the Lord. (eg. Moses, Joshua, Daniel).

So firstly, let's look at 2 Kings 4:3-4 for context. A widowed wife of one of the sons of the prophets had debts but had nothing to pay them with. She cries out to Elisha and he encourages this woman to commit herself in faith to God's provision.
The scripture reads, **"Then he said, 'Go, borrow vessels from everywhere, from all your neighbours - empty vessels; do not gather just a few. And when you have come in, you shall shut the door behind you and your sons; then pour it into all those vessels and set aside the full ones.'"**

We can see that the vessels needed to be empty in order to be filled. And they needed to shut the door, to make it a private place between them and the Lord, and then the vessels were filled. And it was an act of faith!

In the same way, we can come to the Lord IN FAITH knowing that He will meet us in the secret place and is ready and waiting to fill us supernaturally.
Spurgeon says, *"A full Christ is for empty sinners.... It is not our emptiness but our fullness which can hinder the outgoings of free grace"*.
This should lead us to the question, 'what are we filling ourselves with?'

Mark 1:17 says, **"Then Jesus said to them, "Follow Me, and I will make you become fishers of men."**
When Jesus called His disciples, it was like a calling to head out on an apprenticeship with Him. During their time with Him the disciples were constantly learning from Him and imitating Him. One of the things they would have seen Jesus do often was withdraw to quiet places to be with God. If Jesus did that, how much more do we need to do the same.

Withdrawing and developing a relationship with God in secret is important. Matthew 6:5-6 reads, **"And when you pray, you shall not be like the hypocrites. For they love to pray standing in the synagogues and on the corners of the streets, that they may be seen by men... But you, when you pray, go into your room, and when you have shut your door, pray to your Father who is in the secret place;"**
This gives us a great illustration of imitating Christ in this - withdrawing to spend time with God and praying in the secret place.

Interestingly, if we go back and look at Matthew 6: 1-18, Jesus talks about the spiritual disciplines of giving, prayer and fasting.
He talks about giving in Matthew 6:3, **"do not let your left hand know what your right hand is doing"**.
He talks about prayer in verse 5 above, and fasting in Matthew 6:17-18, **"but you, when you fast, anoint your head and wash your face, so that you do not appear to men to be fasting"**.

We can see that the theme of these verses is about developing a life of prayer and worship IN SECRET with the Lord, WITHOUT the motivation of being seen by man.

When the disciples were called they let go of much to immediately go and follow Jesus in obedience to His first command. And we need to do the same.
Claiming to have no time or energy is not an excuse. Time in the secret place with Christ is essential for your walk with Him, as is clearly illustrated throughout scripture. You need to prioritise Him, and TRUST Him to give you what you need as you give Him this time!

As we talked about earlier, the secret place is not necessarily a physical space, but a spiritual state in our relationship with God. You can invite Him into even the mundane daily tasks such as driving, cooking dinner, showering, washing dishes, etc. BUILD it into your life every day, making sure you get to that secret place with Him daily, even making space for extended periods of time, so that you consistently abide in that place. It's what He desires and requests of us; to love and be loved!
1 John 4:19 says, **"we love because He first loved us."** Love is a two-way relationship and time in the secret place really helps us to strip things back and learn to spend quality time with Christ, loving Him, and being loved by Him.

At times it does us good to withdraw to a physical secret place. Jesus often withdrew to the mountain tops or wilderness to be with God (Luke 5:16, Mark 6:46, Luke 6:12).
Jesus himself set the example of withdrawing and spending intimate time with God and it's necessary for us to follow His example. To reiterate the importance - if Jesus himself needed to withdraw and spend time with God, how much more do we!

He is waiting for you to make time and space to be alone with Him, to empty your mind and soul of everything before Him, so He can fill you with His glory - His love, His oil.

When you are filled in the secret place you are able to pour out what you have received into the lives of others.

REFLECTION

A summary of what you learnt in this chapter.

REFLECTION

How does this challenge you personally?

REFLECTION

What is God saying to you personally?

APPLICATION

How will you apply this practically in your life?
(your response to the last reflection question)

PRAYER

Here is a space to journal a prayer or some prayer points based off your reflections and application to this chapter.

DWELLING AND ABIDING

Abiding in His Shadow

Psalm 91:1 **"He who dwells in the secret place of the Most High shall abide under the shadow of the Almighty"**

What does it mean to dwell in the secret place and abide in His shadow?

"Dwells" in Hebrew is *"yasab"* which means to remain, sit, abide, stay, be inhabited, marry, endure (Strong's definitions). These words show us that dwelling in the secret place isn't simply coming and going, it's staying and remaining in that heart space. Abiding is one of the words used to describe that state of 'dwelling'.
In the verse above, it says that we 'shall abide under the shadow of the Almighty'. When I recently did an in-depth study of this, it bought me great revelation and I was able to see the wealth of meaning and power in this passage of scripture!

Let's take a look at *divine overshadowing*.
Acts 5:15 KJV says, **"they brought forth the sick into the streets, and laid them on beds and couches, that at the least the shadow of Peter passing by might overshadow some of them"**

"Overshadow" in Greek is *"episkiazo"* which means to throw shade upon.
Strong's definition says, "to envelop in a haze of brilliancy; figuratively, to invest with preternatural influence: - overshadow".
Thayer's Greek Lexicon says, "a use of the word which seems to have been drawn from the familiar Old Testament idea of a cloud as symbolizing the immediate presence and power of God".
In the "HELPS Word studies" when looking at the word *"episkiazo"* it says *"episkiazo"* ("overshadow") is used in the NT of God's over-shadowing presence – which always brings His boule-plan to pass. "Boule" = "God's immutable (unchanging overtime/unable to be changed) will for physical circumstances".

Unpacking the meaning of these words shows us that there is great power in being under His shadow, in His overshadowing presence, and it brings His immutable will to pass. His desire is for us to dwell in that place, the secret place, and abide under His shadow so that He can accomplish His will in you and through you!

Psalm 121:5 reads, **"The Lord is your keeper; The Lord is your shade at your right hand."** The word "shade" here in Hebrew is *'tsale'* which means defence or, (again) shadow!
The right hand also holds great significance. The ancient Romans and Greeks held their shield in the left hand, and their weapon in their right hand. The right hand was considered the vulnerable side because it had no shield. It was exposed. God often refers to Himself as being at your right hand, which signifies HIS covering and protection!
 Psalm 119:114 reads; **"you are my hiding place and my shield; I hope in Your word"** He is our shield. Our shadow. Our protection. And it is up to us to choose to dwell (abide, remain) in that secret place –"under the shadow of the Almighty."

In Matthew 14 (where Jesus walks on the sea) we are given a great example of what happens when we keep our minds on Him, rather than on the things going on around us. Keeping our mind on Him by dwelling in the secret place, helps us to remain IN Him When we lose focus, we slip away from that place with Him in our hearts.

Matthew 14:22-32 reads, **"Immediately Jesus made His disciples get into the boat and go before Him to the other side, while He sent the multitudes away. And when He had sent the multitudes away, He went up on the mountain by Himself to pray. Now when evening came, He was alone there. But the boat was now in the middle of the sea, tossed by the waves, for the wind was contrary. Now in the fourth watch of the night Jesus went to them, walking on the sea. And when the disciples saw Him walking on the sea, they were troubled, saying, "It is a ghost!" And they cried out for fear. But immediately Jesus spoke to them, saying, "Be of good cheer! It is I; do not be afraid." And Peter answered Him and said, "Lord, if it is You, command me to come to You on the water." So He said, "Come." And when Peter had come down out of the boat, he walked on the water to go to Jesus. But when he saw that the wind was boisterous, he was afraid; and beginning to sink he cried out, saying, "Lord, save me!" And immediately Jesus stretched out His hand and caught him, and said to him, "O you of little faith, why did you doubt?" And when they got into the boat, the wind ceased"**

Interestingly we see here that it was Peter's idea to walk on the water. Jesus simply said, "Come." (essentially, it was Peter's prayer request and Jesus made it happen). When he made the request Peter had his eyes on Jesus, but then, when Jesus made it happen, Peter took his eyes off Jesus by looking at the situation and he began to sink.

We need to keep our eyes focussed on Jesus by maintaining an uninterrupted focus on Him. We need to keep our mind constantly dwelling on Him by allowing our thoughts to be steadfastly centred on His presence, not on the things around us.
To help with this, it is important to ask these questions in our day to day life, *"Where is my focus? What is my mind dwelling on right now?"*

It's also important to note that Jesus stretched out His hand to catch Peter and said, **"O you of little faith, why did you doubt?"**
Dwelling on Jesus, keeping our thoughts and eyes fixed on Him, keeps our faith strong and minimises doubt! This also emphasises the importance of coming to Him in faith! Trusting completely that when you are in continual communion with Him you are truly, continuously living in His presence and understanding what that actually means!

Looking at Psalm 27:4 and 6, it reads, **"One thing I have desired of the LORD, That will I seek: That I may dwell in the house of the LORD All the days of my life, To behold the beauty of the LORD, And to inquire in His temple.**
Therefore I will offer sacrifices of joy in His tabernacle; I will sing, yes, I will sing praises to the LORD"

What we see here is that element of dwelling that involves seeking and sacrifice. This specific verse demonstrates offering sacrifices of praise and joy. We also see the posture of David's heart - he says ONE THING he has DESIRED, that he will SEEK, is to DWELL in the house of the Lord ALL the days of His life.
This really highlights the power of our heart posture and our desires, especially when we look at what David was going through and how his heart posture helped him stay close to Christ by offering up sacrifices of praise and joy despite his circumstances.

Revelation 21:3 reads, **"And I heard a loud voice from heaven saying, "Behold, the tabernacle of God is with men, and He will dwell with them, and they shall be His people. God Himself will be with them and be their God."**
When we invite Christ to come and dwell with us, and when we abide and dwell with Him, we can be confident in faith that we truly are one with Him. This is His desire, for us to abide, dwell, remain in that unity with Him.
To remain one with Him, we need to block out anything that could interfere with our 'view' or vision of Jesus. Think of it as having tunnel vision for Him.
It's our responsibility to seek out what could be blocking our vision of Jesus, so that we can remain one with Him. You will understand the truth of what this means for you when you take the time and make the space to dwell and abide in Him.

Waiting on the Lord

Isaiah 40:31 reads, **"But those who wait on the LORD Shall renew their strength; They shall mount up with wings like eagles, They shall run and not be weary, They shall walk and not faint."**

The word "wait" here in Hebrew is *"qavah"* which means to bind together, collect, gather, look, patiently, tarry, wait for/on/upon (Strongs).

To wait on the Lord doesn't mean doing nothing. To wait on the Lord, means to look for, seek Him out, gather what you can, sit with it, pray over it; not sit around and do nothing. We have a part to play. Nowadays, waiting and patience is harder than ever for us. We like to have things given to us in an instant, and we often want and expect things to happen quickly with as little action from us as necessary.

Another meaning of the word *"qavah"* is to wait expectantly, with hope. So, as we wait on the Lord and we hope and expect Him to move for us; our role is to have faith, to trust Him and to seek Him.

Seeking

The Word of God has so much to say about seeking.
Isaiah 55:6, **"Seek the LORD while He may be found, Call upon Him while He is near."**

1 Chronicles 22:19, **"now set your heart and your soul to seek the Lord your God…"**

1 Chronicles 16:8-13 – vs11 mainly, **"seek the Lord and His strength, Seek His face evermore!"**

Matthew 6:33, **"But seek first the Kingdom and His righteousness and all these things shall be added to you."**

Luke 11:10, **"For everyone who asks receives, and he who seeks finds, and to him who knocks it will be opened."**

Something I've learnt over the years is that we seek Him to find Him. And we need to seek Him with a child-like faith. Think of the game of hide-and-seek - the children go off seeking with so much awe, wonder and excitement! Imagine the joy in the heart of God when we seek Him with that heart posture. When we get to that secret place with Him, imagine the look of joy on His face when we find Him there, and we can actually stay there with Him! It's more like a game of sardines, really!

The main point is that He is waiting for us to seek Him. It is our responsibility to take action. He promises to meet us there and to respond (Matthew 7:7-8, **"Ask, and it will be given to you; seek, and you will find; knock, and it will be opened to you. For everyone who asks receives, and he who seeks finds, and to him who knocks it will be opened."**)

Acts 17:27, **"so that they should seek the Lord, in the hope that they find Him, though He is not far from each one of us;"**

He is SO close to us, just waiting for us to seek him out and just be with Him.

Jeremiah 29:13-14 says, **"And you will seek Me and find Me, when you search for Me with all your heart. I will be found by you, says the LORD, and I will bring you back from your captivity; I will gather you from all the nations and from all the places where I have driven you, says the LORD, and I will bring you to the place from which I cause you to be carried away captive."**

God is a gentleman, and He gives us free-will. He gives us the choice whether to seek Him or not. His promise (if we choose to seek Him) is that we WILL find Him, and nearby. We just have to seek wholeheartedly. Seeking Him wholeheartedly is a significant key. He wants us to be all-in, not just a little bit in!

2 Chronicles 16:9 says, **"For the eyes of the LORD run to and fro throughout the whole earth, to show Himself strong on behalf of those whose heart is loyal to Him."**
Our hearts must seek Him with loyalty, seeking nothing else but Him. We can't have mixed loyalties - seeking the things of the world, as well as seeking the things of the Kingdom. He wants our wholehearted devotion and loyalty to Him and Him alone, just as He deserves. This is also for our protection, and so that He can fulfil His promises to us!

Seeking can simply be looking for Him in the everyday moments - as you look out the window whilst driving, as you walk amongst His incredible creation, as you watch children play, as you stand at the sink washing dishes, as you load the washing machine, as you walk into work, as you wait beside the coffee machine, as you take a bite of lunch. He can be found in even the busiest or most mundane parts of your day if you seek Him in those moments!

He is so kind that you can simply ask Him to reveal Himself to you in that moment, or ask Him to reveal a part His character, or a promise for example, and He will show up! It's important though, as you seek, to be in tune with Him and listening for His gentle whispers that He so graciously places on your heart.

REFLECTION

A summary of what you learnt in this chapter.

REFLECTION

How does this challenge you personally?

REFLECTION

What is God saying to you personally?

APPLICATION

How will you apply this practically in your life?
(your response to the last reflection question)

PRAYER

Here is a space to journal a prayer or some prayer points based off your reflections and application to this chapter.

HOME OF THE HOLY SPIRIT

It's what's Inside that Counts

It's what's on the inside that counts.
A home can have an immaculate garden bed on the outside, but inside be unclean, messy, rundown and not really inviting for someone to dwell in. Sometimes we might look good on the outside, however there's stuff going on in secret, or on the inside of us, that hinders our body being a holy place for the Holy Spirit to dwell in.

Matthew 23:25-28 reads, **"Woe to you, scribes and Pharisees, hypocrites! For you cleanse the outside of the cup and dish, but inside they are full of extortion and self-indulgence. Blind Pharisee, first cleanse the inside of the cup and dish, that the outside of them may be clean also. Woe to you, scribes and Pharisees, hypocrites! For you are like whitewashed tombs which indeed appear beautiful outwardly, but inside are full of dead men's bones and all uncleanness. Even so you also outwardly appear righteous to men, but inside you are full of hypocrisy and lawlessness."**

We really need to evaluate what our home of the Holy Spirit looks like, truly, on the inside. Are we simply maintaining just the garden so that we look good, or are we truly looking after the inside and protecting it from unclean things coming in and creating mess?

Romans 12:1, **"I beseech you therefore, brethren, by the mercies of God, that you present your bodies a living sacrifice, holy, acceptable to God, which is your reasonable service"**.

1 Corinthians 3:16-17, **"Do you not know that you are the temple of God and that the Spirit of God dwells in you? If anyone defiles the temple of God, God will destroy him. For the temple is holy, which temple you are."**

We literally house the Holy Spirit inside of us. We need to understand that, and really grasp it. We must protect the Holy Spirit. God is so pure and doesn't deserve anything but purity! Whatever we expose ourselves to, we're exposing the Holy Spirit to. Our bodies are a temple of the Living God, and we need to honour and respect that truth; really taking it seriously.

1 Corinthians 6:19-20, **"Or do you not know that your body is the temple of the Holy Spirit who is in you, whom you have from God, and you are not your own? For you were bought at a price; therefore glorify God in your body and in your spirit, which are God's."**

God sent His precious son, Jesus Christ to die for you, and He gives you the Holy Spirit to dwell inside of you. He bought you for an incredible price and He deserves nothing less than to be housed in a pure vessel.

"It will be very beneficial to us Christians to study the instructions God gave to Moses when he was setting up the Tabernacle [the place of meeting] in Exodus (Exodus 24-40) . You will see how much detail God put into the Tabernacle just because it was a meeting place for Him and His people. God put the same detail into creating you and saving you. This same God has now chosen your body as His dwelling place. It will help you understand better what it means for Christ Jesus to dwell in your heart. What it means to carry the Spirit of God in your earthly vessel. You and I did not merit it but it was God who chose to make our vessels His dwelling place. You were bought with a price and your body does not belong to you anymore. Your role is like that of the priests of old, to keep the temple holy and fit for God to dwell in."
- written by Fresh Fire Devotional, https://gfhlive.tv/freshfire/2012/09/30/housing-the-holy-spirit/)

1 Peter 1:15-16, **"but as He who called you is holy, you also be holy in all your conduct, because it is written, "Be holy, for I am holy"."**

Purity involves maintaining loyalty to the Holy Spirit – prioritising Him and protecting Him.

John 17:17, **"sanctify them by Your truth, Your word is truth."**
This is a phrase spoken by Jesus when He was praying for His disciples. We know His Word, the Bible, is truth and we know it sanctifies us. It shows us how to live. We can use it as a tool, like a mirror. If we are called to be like Christ, we should act like Christ! And we know that we begin to act like the people that we spend most of our time with.

Ephesians 5:25-27, **"just as Christ also loved the church and gave Himself for her, that He might sanctify and cleanse her with the washing of water by** the word, that He might present her to Himself a glorious church, not having spot or wrinkle or any such thing, but that she should be holy and without blemish."

In this passage Paul gives us a picture of what washing yourself with the Word and living in His love looks like – it purifies us!

Exodus 23:7, **"Keep yourself far from a false matter; do not kill the innocent and righteous. For I will not justify the wicked"**

An innocent person is righteous and is measured by the demands of the law. The spiritual law tells us to keep ourselves FAR from false matter!

Matthew 5:8, **"Blessed are the pure in heart, For they shall see God."**

There are some beautiful promises in the scriptures for us if we choose to be obedient to the call to a life of purity! We all desire to see Him. We seek His face because we love Him. The Bible says the PURE in heart are BLESSED, for they shall see God! That is our desire, and that is His desire too. It's purity that helps us get to that place.

Colossians 1:11-14, **"We also pray that you will be strengthened with all his glorious power so you will have all the endurance and patience you need. May you be filled with joy, always thanking the Father. He has enabled you to share in the inheritance that belongs to his people, who live in the light. For he has rescued us from the kingdom of darkness and transferred us into the Kingdom of his dear Son, who purchased our freedom and forgave our sins."**

There is an inheritance for those who live in the light. We have been transferred out of darkness, into the light, and we need to stay in the light! There is blessing when we do that. Jesus DIED for our freedom so we could be presented spotless, blameless before the Lord, as children of God. We really need to honour what He did!

(Jude 1:24, **"Now to Him who is able to keep you from stumbling, And to present you faultless Before the presence of His glory with exceeding joy"**)

2 Timothy 2:21, **"Therefore if anyone cleanses himself from the latter, he will be a vessel for honour, sanctified and useful for the Master, prepared for every good work."**

This same scripture above in the NLT version really captures this well, which reads, **"If you keep yourself pure, you will be a special utensil for honourable use. Your life will be clean, and you will be ready for the Master to use you for every good work."**

Being cleansed, then remaining pure, allows us to be an honourable vessel for Christ to use. To be used as a vessel for Christ is part of the great commission!

SCRIPTURES FOR US TO PONDER AND PRAY FROM:

-Psalm 51:10-12, **"Create in me a clean heart, O God, And renew a steadfast spirit within me. Do not cast me away from Your presence, And do not take Your Holy Spirit from me. Restore to me the joy of Your salvation, And uphold me by Your generous Spirit."**

-James 4:7-10, **"Therefore submit to God. Resist the devil and he will flee from you. Draw near to God and He will draw near to you. Cleanse your hands, you sinners; and purify your hearts, you double-minded. Lament and mourn and weep! Let your laughter be turned to mourning and your joy to gloom. Humble yourselves in the sight of the Lord, and He will lift you up."**

REFLECTION

A summary of what you learnt in this chapter.

REFLECTION

How does this challenge you personally?

REFLECTION

What is God saying to you personally?

APPLICATION

How will you apply this practically in your life?
(your response to the last reflection question)

PRAYER

Here is a space to journal a prayer or some prayer points based off your reflections and application to this chapter.

LIVING IN PURITY

Keeping our Eyes, Ears & Minds Pure

What is inside of us is what flows out and we know there is so much power in our words!

We need to be so careful to ensure that all the things that enter our eyes and our ears, and the things that we allow our mind to dwell on, are holy and pure!

Let's explore the dictionary meaning of purity. The Oxford dictionary definition of purity is *"freedom from adulteration or contamination"*,
The Cambridge dictionary definition of purity is *"(NOT MIXED) ; the state of not being mixed with anything else"*
The Collins dictionary definition of purity is *"the condition or quality of being pure; freedom from anything that debases, contaminates, pollutes, etc"* or *"freedom from any admixture or modifying addition"*

The blood of Jesus is pure and it cleanses us from unrighteousness and it's important to stay that way by not allowing anything to come in and contaminate that. The devil throws all sorts of things at us through the world to try and tempt us or lure us into things that contaminate us, and we need to shield ourselves from it.

Isaiah 33:15-16, **"He who walks righteously and speaks uprightly, He who despises the gain of oppressions, Who gestures with his hands, refusing bribes, Who stops his ears from hearing of bloodshed, And shuts his eyes from seeing evil: He will dwell on high; His place of defence will be the fortress of rocks; Bread will be given him, His water will be sure."**

We are simply in the world, we are not OF the world (Romans 12:2 and John 15:19). We are called to be set apart, to be different; this is to keep us pure or 'unmixed'!
For example, if we have our eyes on Jesus, but our ears tuned into unclean music, that is being "mixed". We are to live like the royalty we are in Christ Jesus and live in such a pure way that our lives bring nothing but glory to God.

Hebrews 12:1-3, **"Therefore we also, since we are surrounded by so great a cloud of witnesses, let us lay aside every weight, and the sin which so easily ensnares us, and let us run with endurance the race that is set before us, looking unto Jesus, the author and finisher of our faith, who for the joy that was set before Him endured the cross, despising the shame, and has sat down at the right hand of the throne of God. For consider Him who endured such hostility from sinners against Himself, lest you become weary and discouraged in your souls."**
The phrase "looking unto Jesus" really captures my attention as it really is so important to keep our eyes pure and focussed on Him!

The other part of this scripture that really captures my attention is how we are told to **'lay aside the sin, which EASILY ensnares us'** – we need to lay it aside, take it away, remove it from our lives. The Word itself tells us how easy it is for sin to ensnare us and that we need to have nothing to do with it! Not even the tip of our toe dipped in!
We'll explore this further when we unpack living as children of light, but having nothing to do with the sin that Christ died to set us free from is such an important aspect of purity.

OUR EYES AND EARS:
Matthew 6:22-23, **"The lamp of the body is the eye. If therefore your eye is good, your whole body will be full of light. But if your eye is bad, your whole body will be full of darkness. If therefore the light that is in you is darkness, how great is that darkness!"**
This piece of scripture shows us that there is great power in the eye (in other words, in what we look at).

Another great scripture in line with this is Matthew 5:28 which gives us a convincing example of how serious we need to take the power of the eye. It reads; **"But I say to you that whoever looks at a woman to lust for her has already committed adultery with her in his heart."** – a simple look with lust is the same as committing adultery. Our eyes hold that much power over the purity of our bodies. As children of God we need to do everything we can to keep our eyes pure!
Psalm 119:37 says, **"Turn away my eyes from looking at worthless things, And revive me in Your way."**

The things that don't honour the Kingdom of Heaven, even if they aren't necessarily "sin" at first glance, are things we need to turn our eyes away from. As we read earlier, sin creeps up on us and ensnares us so easily; so if something doesn't bring honour to the Kingdom of God, turn your eyes away. We need to revive ourselves in His way through the Word and have eyes only for Him.

Proverbs 4:20-22, **"My son, give attention to my words; Incline your ear to my sayings. Do not let them depart from your eyes; Keep them in the midst of your heart; For they are life to those who find them, And health to all their flesh."**

"God tells us to guard what we hear, what we see, and what is in our hearts. He wants us to have our ears full of the gracious words of Jesus, our eyes full of the presence of Jesus and our hearts meditating on what we have heard and seen in Jesus." (Joseph Prince)

OUR MIND
Philippians 4:8-9, **"Finally, brethren, whatever things are true, whatever things are noble, whatever things are just, whatever things are pure, whatever things are lovely, whatever things are of good report, if there is any virtue and if there is anything praiseworthy—meditate on these things. The things which you learned and received and heard and saw in me, these do, and the God of peace will be with you."**

Renewing our mind with His Word and dwelling in His presence helps us to stay pure.
We need to protect our whole body, particularly importantly our eyes, ears and mind. Take captive and turn away from everything that is unholy and doesn't bring Him glory and honour. We need to be filling every fibre of our being with His truths, with things that are pure, that grow us spiritually and encourage us in our walk with Jesus.

Living as Children of Light

There are many scriptures to look at in regard to living as children of light.
Living as children of light means living in the light of Christ, rather than in darkness.

We come into the light through the revelation of His Word, and then living it out!
Psalm 119:9-12, **"How can a young man cleanse his way? By taking heed according to Your word. With my whole heart I have sought You; Oh, let me not wander from Your commandments! Your word I have hidden in my heart, That I might not sin against You. Blessed are You, O Lord! Teach me Your statutes."**

The following are some key scriptures regarding being the light of Christ that we must have revelation of and live out in our everyday lives.

- Isaiah 60:1-3 shows us the importance for the nations that we as believers are truly living in LIGHT!

"Arise, shine; For your light has come! And the glory of the LORD is risen upon you. For behold, the darkness shall cover the earth, And deep darkness the people; But the LORD will arise over you, And His glory will be seen upon you. The Gentiles shall come to your light, And kings to the brightness of your rising."

We can liken this to having an oil lamp inside of us; when we come to Christ in repentance and give our lives to Him, it's as though He lights that lamp inside of us and we no longer walk in darkness and can therefore be a light to others. They are drawn to the light because the darkness causes them to continually stumble in life. Once He lights up that oil lamp inside us, it is our responsibility to keep it alight by constantly collecting oil through intimacy with Him.. When we make choices and do things in alignment with the darkness, the light diminishes bit by bit.... intimacy keeps us from darkness. This is a really important key, and we will unpack the oil in greater detail later! But keeping the lamp alight, and specifically shining the light, is what we will focus on here.

- Philippians 2:14-15 says, **"Do all things without complaining and disputing, that you may become blameless and harmless, children of God without fault in the midst of a crooked and perverse generation, among whom you shine as lights in the world."**

This shows we need to be blameless and harmless. As we shine our lights in the world we are setting the example and representing Jesus to others who are drawn to Him by our light.

- Colossians 1:12 says, **"giving thanks to the Father who has qualified us to be partakers of the inheritance of the saints in the light."**

Giving thanks is another key to shining your light. As we come to Christ with a heart posture of gratitude, we are lit up even brighter on the inside! And how can we not have a heart posture of gratitude?! Christ has QUALIFIED us to be partakers of the inheritance of the saints in the light! There is inheritance for us when we live this way, and He has qualified us for it! When we truly grasp this truth it becomes more real to us and we will consequently naturally give thanks and posture our hearts that way.

The book of Ephesians is a great book to read in regard to what it looks like to walk as children of light, as is the book of James. You can read through these books in your own time, but for now let's look at some pieces of scripture that I find key:

Ephesians 4:17 - 5:21

"This I say, therefore, and testify in the Lord, that you should no longer walk as the rest of the Gentiles walk, in the futility of their mind, having their understanding darkened, being alienated from the life of God, because of the ignorance that is in them, because of the blindness of their heart; who, being past feeling, have given themselves over to lewdness, to work all uncleanness with greediness.
But you have not so learned Christ, if indeed you have heard Him and have been taught by Him, as the truth is in Jesus: that you put off, concerning your former conduct, the old man which grows corrupt according to the deceitful lusts, and be renewed in the spirit of your mind, and that you put on the new man which was created according to God, in true righteousness and holiness.

Therefore, putting away lying, "Let each one of you speak truth with his neighbour," for we are members of one another. "Be angry, and do not sin": do not let the sun go down on your wrath, nor give place to the devil. Let him who stole steal no longer, but rather let him labour, working with his hands what is good, that he may have something to give him who has need. Let no corrupt word proceed out of your mouth, but what is good for necessary edification, that it may impart grace to the hearers. And do not grieve the Holy Spirit of God, by whom you were sealed for the day of redemption. Let all bitterness, wrath, anger, clamour, and evil speaking be put away from you, with all malice. And be kind to one another, tenderhearted, forgiving one another, even as God in Christ forgave you.

Therefore, be imitators of God as dear children. And walk in love, as Christ also has loved us and given Himself for us, an offering and a sacrifice to God for a sweet-smelling aroma. But fornication and all uncleanness or covetousness, let it not even be named among you, as is fitting for saints; neither filthiness, nor foolish talking, nor coarse jesting, which are not fitting, but rather giving of thanks. For this you know, that no fornicator, unclean person, nor covetous man, who is an idolater, has any inheritance in the kingdom of Christ and God.

Let no one deceive you with empty words, for because of these things the wrath of God comes upon the sons of disobedience. Therefore, do not be partakers with them. For you were once darkness, but now you are light in the Lord. Walk as children of light (for the fruit of the Spirit is in all goodness, righteousness, and truth), finding out what is acceptable to the Lord. And have no fellowship with the unfruitful works of darkness, but rather expose them. For it is shameful even to speak of those things which are done by them in secret. But all things that are exposed are made manifest by the light, for whatever makes manifest is light.

Therefore He says: "Awake, you who sleep, Arise from the dead, And Christ will give you light."

See then that you walk circumspectly, not as fools but as wise, redeeming the time, because the days are evil.
Therefore do not be unwise, but understand what the will of the Lord is. And do not be drunk with wine, in which is dissipation; but be filled with the Spirit, speaking to one another in psalms and hymns and spiritual songs, singing and making melody in your heart to the Lord, giving thanks always for all things to God the Father in the name of our Lord Jesus Christ, submitting to one another in the fear of God."

This passage gives us a wonderful picture of what it looks like to walk as children of light before Christ; it means setting the example of holiness, and truly loving like Jesus.

I'd like to highlight Ephesians 5:8-14 which in my bible has the subheading of "Walk in the Light" and interestingly mentions the fruit of the Spirit.

"For you were once darkness, but now you are light in the Lord. Walk as children of light (for the fruit of the Spirit is in all goodness, righteousness, and truth), finding out what is acceptable to the Lord. And have no fellowship with the unfruitful works of darkness, but rather expose them. For it is shameful even to speak of those things which are done by them in secret. But all things that are exposed are made manifest by the light, for whatever makes manifest is light. Therefore He says: "Awake, you who sleep, Arise from the dead, And Christ will give you light."

The fruit of the Spirit are significant here. We can continually meditate and reflect on them as a valuable guide for how to shape our character and behaviour to be like Christ. These are the things that are acceptable to the Lord, and the standard for walking in the light.

A summary of what you learnt in this chapter.

REFLECTION

How does this challenge you personally?

REFLECTION

What is God saying to you personally?

APPLICATION

How will you apply this practically in your life?
(your response to the last reflection question)

PRAYER

Here is a space to journal a prayer or some prayer points based off your reflections and application to this chapter.

THE OIL OF INTIMACY

The Oil

In the previous section, I said that, metaphorically speaking, we have a lamp inside of us and when we come to Christ in repentance and give our lives to Him, it's like He lights that lamp on the inside of us, and we no longer walk in darkness and can therefore be a light to others. They are drawn to the light because their darkness causes them to continually stumble in life, and our light often looks appealing and helpful to them in their situations; it can act like a magnet!
I explained that once The Lord lights up that oil lamp inside of us it is our responsibility to continue collecting oil through intimacy with Him to keep it alight.

Oil is often referred to in scripture as the oil of intimacy. We see a clear explanation of this in Matthew 25 where Jesus shares The Parable of the Wise and Foolish Virgins.

Matthew 25:1-13
"**Then the kingdom of heaven shall be likened to ten virgins who took their lamps and went out to meet the bridegroom. Now five of them were wise, and five were foolish. Those who were foolish took their lamps and took no oil with them, but the wise took oil in their vessels with their lamps. But while the bridegroom was delayed, they all slumbered and slept. "And at midnight a cry was heard: 'Behold, the bridegroom is coming; go out to meet him!' Then all those virgins arose and trimmed their lamps. And the foolish said to the wise, 'Give us some of your oil, for our lamps are going out.' But the wise answered, saying, 'No, lest there should not be enough for us and you; but go rather to those who sell, and buy for yourselves.' And while they went to buy, the bridegroom came, and those who were ready went in with him to the wedding; and the door was shut. "Afterward the other virgins came also, saying, 'Lord, Lord, open to us!' But he answered and said, 'Assuredly, I say to you, I do not know you.' "Watch therefore, for you know neither the day nor the hour in which the Son of Man is coming."**

The young women who were caught unprepared, without enough oil, were denied entry to the wedding feast. We know that we are awaiting Jesus' return and waiting to feast with Him at the marriage supper of the Lamb (Revelations 19:9 **"Then he said to me, "Write: 'Blessed are those who are called to the marriage supper of the Lamb!' " And he said to me, "These are the true sayings of God."**)

The virgins who had no oil were calling out to the Lord to open the door and let them in, but the Lord answers them saying, **"Assuredly, I say to you, I do not know you."**
The Lord saying to those without the oil, **"I do not know you"**.

We see something similar in Matthew 7:21-23 which reads, **"Not everyone who says to Me, 'Lord, Lord,' shall enter the kingdom of heaven, but he who does the will of My Father in heaven. Many will say to Me in that day, 'Lord, Lord, have we not prophesied in Your name, cast out demons in Your name, and done many wonders in Your name?' And then I will declare to them, 'I never knew you; depart from Me, you who practice lawlessness!'"**

Intimacy with the Lord is EVERYTHING. We need that oil of intimacy; it is literally a matter of life and death.

It's important to understand that our works are not what produce oil, it's our intimacy; a deep and meaningful relationship with the Lord, that produces oil.

We know that to make olive oil for instance, the olives need to go through a process of pressing and refining to make pure oil. Much like this, our relationship with God is a process of being pressed and refined to be purified!

Understanding the importance of oil in regard to intimacy with God is one thing, but actually living it out is another. Luke 12, which we will explore soon, talks about keeping our lamps burning and being ready for service. To keep the lamp burning we need oil; in other words we need intimacy with God every single day. It should be the one, non-negotiable thing that we do every day no matter what - our first and highest priority.

Keeping the lamp burning

Leviticus 6:12-13, **"And the fire on the altar shall be kept burning on it; it shall not be put out. And the priest shall burn wood on it every morning, and lay the burnt offering in order on it; and he shall burn on it the fat of the peace offerings. A fire shall always be burning on the altar; it shall never go out."**

The Enduring Word Commentary suggests, *"The long-burning character of the burnt offering is an appropriate illustration of the work of giving ourselves completely to God."* And Clarke quotes, *"Does the perpetual fire burn on the altar of thy heart? Art thou ever looking unto Jesus, and beholding, by faith, the Lamb of God which taketh away the sin of the world?"*

It's interesting to note that Leviticus 9:24 tells us that the altar's fire was ignited by a fire that miraculously came from the Lord, which contributed to the reason why the altar's fire should not be allowed to go out. It was God's fire and was to be cared for and respected.

John Trapp, when reflecting on the fact that the fire of the altar should not go out, said, *"No more should our faith, love, zeal (that flame of God, as Solomon calls it, Song of Solomon 8:6-7), that should never go out; the waters should not quench it, nor the ashes cover it."*

Leviticus 24:1-4 reads, **""Then the Lord spoke to Moses, saying: "Command the children of Israel that they bring to you pure oil of pressed olives for the light, to make the lamps burn continually. Outside the veil of the Testimony, in the tabernacle of meeting, Aaron shall be in charge of it from evening until morning before the Lord continually; it shall be a statute forever in your generations. He shall be in charge of the lamps on the pure gold lamp-stand before the Lord continually."**

The tabernacle's only source of light were the lamps standing on the solid gold lampstand. If we read Exodus 25:31-40, we can see the detail in the lamp stands and what was needed for them. We can also see that they had to be cared for, which involved trimming their wicks and making sure there was an uninterrupted supply of pure olive oil. It was because of this care that they burned continuously. God did not want a tabernacle left in darkness which was the reason why it was so important that the light from the oil lamps shone continuously.

Similarly, we are to burn continuously to be a light in the world as Jesus was (John 8:12 **"Then Jesus spoke to them again, saying, "I am the light of the world. He who follows Me shall not walk in darkness, but have the light of life.""**)

To remain continuously burning for Jesus we need to maintain the fire inside of us which He miraculously lights up when we give our lives to Him, just as the lamps and the fire on the altar had to be maintained. We maintain the fire with the oil - the oil of intimacy!

Another example in scripture from the New Testament of keeping your lamps burning is found in Luke 12:35-38, which reads, **"Let your waist be girded and your lamps burning; and you yourselves be like men who wait for** their master, when he will return from the wedding, that when he comes and knocks they may open to him immediately. Blessed are those servants whom the master, when he comes, will find watching. Assuredly, I say to you that he will gird himself and have them sit down to eat, and will come and serve them. And if he should come in the second watch, or come in the third watch, and find them so, blessed are those servants."**

The picture painted here can be likened to an army lieutenant being ready for service. He is always in training and always on call, ready for action at any moment. In the same way we are to be ready for the return of Christ at any moment!

When we look at the word "girded" in this scripture, the Greek word is: *perizonnymi* –which means to fasten garments with a girdle or belt. Or sometimes used as a metaphor with truth as a girdle *"to equip oneself with the knowledge of truth"* This immediately brings the belt of truth to mind for me and highlights the importance of God's Word as an essential part of keeping our lamps burning. (Matthew 4:4 **"But He answered and said, "It is written, 'Man shall not live by bread alone, but by every word that proceeds from the mouth of God.'"**)

The Word of God brings us into deeper intimacy with Him. We can't just have it in our heads though, we need it written on our hearts which comes from intimate time in communion with the author!

Tunnel Vision

Matthew 6:22 [KJV] reads, **"The light of the body is the eye: if therefore thine eye be single, thy whole body shall be full of light."**

The first thing that jumps out as I read this is that the eye, 'being single', leads to a whole body being full of light; this to me looks like having tunnel vision for the Lord and His ways. Having tunnel vision, or a single eye on Christ alone, means to have Him exclusively in the centre of your view; your focus fully on Him alone.
Placing full focus on God means blocking out anything that prevents from Him being in the front and centre of your view.

Hebrews 12:2, "looking unto Jesus, the author and finisher of our faith, who for the joy that was set before Him endured the cross, despising the shame, and has sat down at the right hand of the throne of God."

When we look to Jesus, setting our eyes upon Him as our focus and our example, we are able to run the race set before us with endurance!! (Hebrews 12:1). Setting our eyes upon Him is a key aspect of having the ability to do life with Him well.

In Ancient Greek, "looking unto Jesus" means looking away from other things and looking unto, or towards, Jesus.
"The Greek word for 'looking' is a much richer word than we can find in the English language. The word is 'aphoraō' which means to turn the eyes away from other things and fix them on something else. We are to look away from all other things and fix our eyes on Jesus.

"Do not even look upon the racecourse, or the competitors, but look to Jesus and so start in the race." (Spurgeon)

2 Corinthians 4:18 [NIV] **"So we fix our eyes not on what is seen, but on what is unseen, since what is seen is temporary, but what is unseen is eternal."**

When we fix our eyes on what is unseen, we gain a fresh, heavenly perspective that is in alignment with the Word and will of God, instead of an earthly perspective. Having a heavenly perspective builds our faith and trust in Christ which strengthens our relationship with Him.

Psalm 16:8 [NIV], **"I keep my eyes always on the Lord. With him at my right hand, I will not be shaken."**
The NKJV reads, **"I have set the Lord always before me; Because He is at my right hand I shall not be moved."**

David made a decision to always 'set' God first in his life, making God his focus.
To strengthen himself when struggles arose David tried his best to keep a constant sense of the Lord's presence and victory in his sight. The Lord and the truth of His Word was David's focus; this was what he chose to keep his eyes on.

Through the life of David we see that this focus is an essential part of our walk with Christ and we need to do the same. It's what gives us that heavenly perspective which we need to maintain in order not to lose focus or hope.

Part of having our eyes on Him and Him alone means we have to make some changes in our lives to ensure our eyes are not swayed or do not lose focus. This means removing distractions and prioritising Him. If Satan can't make you sin, he will try to distract you. Distraction can look innocent; even good at times, (such as, for e.g., an intensive Bible study or discipling someone), however this may take away time from you for just being still and spending intimate, quality time with Christ.

Having the right people in your life for accountability is an important way to keep your focus - maintaining tunnel vision for Christ alone, and not allowing distraction to creep in!

A summary of what you learnt in this chapter.

REFLECTION

How does this challenge you personally?

REFLECTION

What is God saying to you personally?

APPLICATION

How will you apply this practically in your life?
(your response to the last reflection question)

PRAYER

Here is a space to journal a prayer or some prayer points based off your reflections and application to this chapter.

LOVING

Loving Well

People can tell when love is genuine. Love coming from a place of intimacy and purity in Christ produces genuine, and authentic love. We need to authentically love God, AND others! The loving God part is often easy when you grasp His love for you, however, loving others can often be a challenge. When our hearts are in the right place and authentically abiding in intimacy and purity in the Lord, we are able to genuinely love others.

Loving well is not just a suggestion or a helpful thought, it's a command that is so essential to your walk with God that it is repeated many times throughout scripture.
Matthew 22:37 reads, **"Jesus said to him, 'You shall love the LORD your God with all your heart, with all your soul, and with all your mind'."**

Love needs to be shown through every part of your life. We can't say that we love and then not show love practically - love without fruit isn't genuine love because love is more of an action than a feeling.
If we read Romans 12:9-21 Paul explains how love shows itself by our actions. It comes from heart, soul and mind - again, loving with EVERYTHING, with every part of you.

Romans 12:9-21 reads: **"Let love be without hypocrisy. Abhor what is evil. Cling to what is good. Be kindly affectionate to one another with brotherly love, in honor giving preference to one another; not lagging in diligence, fervent in spirit, serving the Lord; rejoicing in hope, patient in tribulation, continuing steadfastly in prayer; distributing to the needs of the saints, given to hospitality. Bless those who persecute you; bless and do not curse. Rejoice with those who rejoice, and weep with those who weep. Be of the same mind toward one another. Do not set your mind on high things, but associate with the humble. Do not be wise in your own opinion. Repay no one evil for evil. Have regard for good things in the sight of all men. If it is possible, as much as depends on** you, live peaceably with all men. Beloved, do not avenge yourselves, but rather give place to wrath; for it is written, "Vengeance is Mine, I will repay," says the Lord. Therefore "If your enemy is hungry, feed him; If he is thirsty, give him a drink; For in so doing you will heap coals of fire on his head." Do not be overcome by evil, but overcome evil with good."**

Love is sacrificial, generous, and shows fruitful, genuine care and love even when you may not feel like it.

Dr Tom Davis noted that "Love is mentioned 714 times in the Bible, yet "giving" or "possessions" is mentioned 2,172 times." The command "love one another" itself is mentioned 11 times in the Bible also.
Love and giving love is not to be taken lightly.

In Revelations 2:1-7 John warns us of what the Lord said of "The Loveless Church" and gives us a great picture of works vs love.

If we look at the church in Ephesus as described in these verses, we can see that they truly did do so many things right, but they had lost their first love for Christ. They are given a warning that if they don't get that love back their lampstand would be removed from them (we know the lampstand represents the church). The whole church would be removed because they had lost their first love despite doing so much well. They knew their doctrine, they didn't put up with sin, they valued holiness, they endured, standing firm in persecution, but their love was gone - the intimate relationship was lost.

Our love for God and our love for others that comes because of our love for Christ, needs to be taken really seriously in the church.

Jude 1:20-21 reads, **"But you, beloved, building yourselves up on your most holy faith, praying in the Holy Spirit, keep yourselves in the love of God, looking for the mercy of our Lord Jesus Christ unto eternal life."**
To keep ourselves in the love of God, we must continue to build ourselves up in faith by intentionally working on growing spiritually.

Another way to keep ourselves in the love of God is through praying in the Holy Spirit, which we will expand on later.

The last point mentioned here is looking for the mercy of Jesus - focusing on the hope of Jesus and what He did for us helps to keep us in that place of gratitude and awe. Meditate on what He did for you at the cross and allow yourself to be drenched in His love so that you have all the love to pour out to others.

Love and Unity

John 17:21-23 reads, "I do not pray for these alone, but also for those who will believe in Me through their word; that they all may be one, as You, Father, are in Me, and I in You; that they also may be one in Us, that the world may believe that You sent Me. And the glory which You gave Me I have given them, that they may be one just as We are one: I in them, and You in Me; that they may be made perfect in one, and that the world may know that You have sent Me, and have loved them as You have loved Me."

Jesus makes note here that He is praying not just for His disciples but for all believers, and expresses His desire for unity in the body of Christ to be likened to His relationship with the Father - being one. This means a connection that is not just superficial, but one that is deep and meaningful!

We can't expect to be unified and 'one' like the Father and Son are one by only attending church on Sundays. Unity and love are built by sharing our lives with one another - by coming together through the week for worship, prayer, by checking in on one another, making meals for each other and by discipling one another in the Word and ways of the Lord.
An important and key aspect of this is LOVE. It is the greatest command and to love others the way we need to, to be truly unified, we need to receive a deep understanding and continual, fresh revelations of the Father's love.

We love because He first loved us (1 John 4:19), and 1 John 4:20-21 says, **"If someone says, "I love God," and hates his brother, he is a liar; for he who does not love his brother whom he has seen, how can he love God whom he has not seen? And this commandment we have from Him: that he who loves God must love his brother also."**

In order to do unity well we need to love well, and in order to love well we need a deep, intimate relationship with the Lord to truly KNOW love. We need to be filled with His love in order to pour out His love. What we are filled with, is what will pour out of us!

To truly grasp the Father's love, we need to truly know Him, and so we need to spend quality time with Him, devouring His Word, and engaging in daily prayer and worship.

A summary of what you learnt in this chapter.

REFLECTION

How does this challenge you personally?

REFLECTION

What is God saying to you personally?

APPLICATION

How will you apply this practically in your life?
(your response to the last reflection question)

PRAYER

Here is a space to journal a prayer or some prayer points based off your reflections and application to this chapter.

WORSHIP AND PRAYER

Daily Worship

Acts 13:22, **"'I have found David the son of Jesse, a man after My own heart, who will do all My will.'"**

Imagine God saying this about you. That is one of our deep desires. David was known as one who deeply understood what it was to love and worship God and the importance of an intimate relationship with God. Throughout the scriptures we see that David would worship and glorify the Lord in all situations; it was like a weapon in his battles and showed great humility. It also showed his reverence and awe of God. Looking at the life of David we can see how important it is to have our hearts posture in the right place. It also shows God that we are humble, open and devoted to Him.

Psalm 63:1-5, **"O God, You are my God; Early will I seek You; My soul thirsts for You; My flesh longs for You In a dry and thirsty land Where there is no water. So I have looked for You in the sanctuary, To see Your power and Your glory. Because Your lovingkindness is better than life, My lips shall praise You. Thus I will bless You while I live; I will lift up my hands in Your name. My soul shall be satisfied as with marrow and fatness, And my mouth shall praise You with joyful lips."**

David was vulnerable in the way He conversed with God, and would freely pour his heart out, then lift God up and honour Him and praise Him. He would seek Him early in the day which showed an eagerness as well as showing that God was his first priority and the only One Who would satisfy and sustain him when there was nothing else available to him.

Spurgeon has some great quotes about David from these verses including:
- *"There was no desert in his heart, though there was a desert around him."*

- *"Learn from this, and do not say, 'I will get into communion with God when I feel better,' but long for communion now. It is one of the temptations of the devil to tell you not to pray when you do not feel like praying. Pray twice as much then."*
- *"David sought God at the tabernacle to connect in some way with God's power and glory. Significantly, David was not at the tabernacle when he sang this song; he was in the Wilderness of Judah. Yet he knew that God's sanctuary was not only a place, but also a spiritual concept that could be entered by faith no matter where a person was."*

The last quote really encapsulates the fact that the Secret Place, the sanctuary of God, is always accessible anywhere, anytime. We simply have to come before Him. These days we have so many distractions and excuses that pull us away from worshipping God and spending time with Him. Yet David's example is one to live by. He was probably quite lonely and had many reasons for worry during his time out in the wilderness, but none of his feelings or worries stopped him from worshipping. He kept his eyes focussed on God rather than on his situation or circumstances. He gave his feelings, thoughts and situations to God, and then he gave God glory, declaring what he knew was God's truth.

We need to choose to praise and worship God every day no matter how we feel. In fact, worship is warfare and it can completely change and shift our mood and circumstances, keeping our eyes fixed on God who is so worthy of nothing less!

Coming before God

Exodus 33:8-10, **"So it was, whenever Moses went out to the tabernacle, that all the people rose, and each man stood at his tent door and watched Moses until he had gone into the tabernacle. And it came to pass, when Moses entered the tabernacle, that the pillar of cloud descended and stood at the door of the tabernacle, and the Lord talked with Moses. All the people saw the pillar of cloud standing at the tabernacle door, and all the people rose and worshiped, each man in his tent door."**

When Moses was going to meet with God the people were in such awe and filled with amazement that a man could truly be meeting with God! They would rise and worship which was such a beautiful response considering that it wasn't even they themselves, but Moses, who was meeting with God. Yet WE, you and I, GET to meet with the King of Kings; we GET to come before Him and communicate with Him. When we truly grasp this, we see that we too should be filled with that same amazement and come before Him boldly, in love, reverence and awe! We get to enter into the Holy place with Christ by the blood of Jesus and talk with GOD! This is our reality!

When we come before God, we can be sure that He is there, listening and ready to communicate with us!

Psalm 6:8-9 says, **"For the LORD has heard the voice of my weeping. The LORD has heard my supplication; The LORD will receive my prayer."**

Philippians 4:6-7 again confirms that God responds when we come before Him with prayer, supplication and thanksgiving!

It reads: **"Be anxious for nothing, but in everything by prayer and supplication, with thanksgiving, let your requests be made known to God; and the peace of God, which surpasses all understanding, will guard your hearts and minds through Christ Jesus."**

God knows our needs, but He wants to hear from us! A one-way relationship is never nice and it's the same with our relationship with Christ; it's all about communication!

Prayer

Prayer is one way we communicate with God.

Two prayers in the Bible that give us a great outline of how to pray are:

1. **"In this manner, therefore, pray: Our Father in heaven, Hallowed be Your name. Your kingdom come. Your will be done on earth as it is in heaven. Give us this day our daily bread. And forgive us our debts, As we forgive our debtors. And do not lead us into temptation, But deliver us from the evil one. For Yours is the kingdom and the power and the glory forever. Amen."**

    -**Our Father in Heaven**: this recognises whom we are praying to, the Almighty God, who is Father; it also highlights the privileged relationship we have.

    - **Hallowed be Your name. Your Kingdom come. Your will be done on earth as it is in heaven**: this shows a appeal for God's glory, it emphasises His agenda and declares that His name, Kingdom and will come first, and are the top priority!

    - **Give us this day our daily bread. And forgive us our debts, as we forgive our debtors. And do not lead us into temptation, but deliver us from the evil one:** This demonstrates bringing our needs to God and trusting Him for our provision. It shows that we acknowledge our need for His provision, forgiveness and strength and seek Him for it.

    - **For Yours is the kingdom and the power and the glory forever**: this shows our praise, our worship, our agreement and credit to Him and His kingdom and his agendas.

2. Ephesians 3; Paul's prayer for the Ephesian Christians (Ephesians 3:14-19)
"For this reason I bow my knees to the Father of our Lord Jesus Christ, from whom the whole family in heaven and earth is named, that He would grant you, according to the riches of His glory, to be strengthened with might through His Spirit in the inner man, that Christ may dwell in your hearts through faith; that you, being rooted and grounded in love, may be able to comprehend with all the saints what is the width and length and depth and height— to know the love of Christ which passes knowledge; that you may be filled with all the fullness of God."

This prayer in Ephesians 3 teaches us to go deeper, praying for the INNER things, rather than circumstances, and praying according to God's will and purposes.
It also teaches us ways we can be praying the will of God over others.

Praying in the Holy Spirit

Another key scripture that teaches us about praying is Jude 1:20 which reads: **"But you, beloved, building yourselves up on your most holy faith, praying in the Holy Spirit,"**

This verse shows us that praying in the Holy Spirit is a key for building faith and building yourself up spiritually, overcoming our flesh and lifting our Spirit! Our prayers are often directed by our own needs, or our own thoughts, or our own wishes and desires, or sometimes we simply can't find the words to pray. There is a higher level of prayer when we pray in the Holy Spirit!

Romans 8:26-27 reads: **"Likewise the Spirit also helps in our weaknesses. For we do not know what we should pray for as we ought, but the Spirit Himself makes intercession for us with groanings which cannot be uttered. Now He who searches the hearts knows what the mind of the Spirit is, because He makes intercession for the saints according to the will of God."**

Praying in the Holy Spirit allows us to communicate with God in a way that is beyond our own knowledge or capacity to articulate our heart before God.

In 1 Corinthians 14:18 Paul says, **"I thank my God I speak with tongues more than you all;"** reiterating the importance and value of praying in the Spirit.

There are also a few things we can learn about prayer from Nehemiah chapter 1.
Nehemiah gives us a great example of what our response should be to circumstances beyond our control, and our response to the things that grieve God.

In Nehemiah 1:4 we read, **"So it was, when I heard these words, that I sat down and wept, and mourned for many days; I was fasting and praying before the God of heaven."**
Nehemiah had just heard about the state of Jerusalem and that they were in great distress and his first and immediate response was to fast and pray. He saw the situation through the eyes of Christ and had a Christ-like response.
Verses 5-11 show us Nehemiah's prayer. We can see that he prays day and night, which demonstrates:
-persistence in prayer
-consistency in prayer life
-commitment to God
-giving and sacrificing time and energy

We can also see that Nehemiah fasts (we will unpack this later), confesses sins, and asks God to remember a promise. And Nehemiah speaks out that promise in prayer. These are key things that we can learn from for our own prayer life!

Worship and Positioning Yourself Physically

Posturing yourself physically as you worship and pray is significant. There are a few different postures in the scriptures that we can look at:
· Bowing - Exodus 34:8, Philippians 2:10, Psalm 95:6
· Kneeling - 2 Chronicles 6:13, Daniel 6:10, Mark 1:40
· Lying prostrate – Deuteronomy 9:25, Matthew 26:39, 1 Corinthians 14:25 (the Greek word for 'worship' is 'proskuneo' which means "prostrate oneself in homage")
· Lifted hands - Psalm 141:2, 1 Timothy 2:8
· Lifted eyes - John 11:41, Luke 9:16
· Silence - Psalm 46:10, 1 Samuel 1:13
· Lifted Voices - Acts 4:24, Psalm 77:1
· Crying out - Psalm 55:17, Hebrew 5:7 (crying out is heartfelt, intense, loud prayer with deep emotion)

Worship

The dictionary definition for worship is *"the feeling or expression of reverence and adoration for a deity"*.
Our worship is how we show God our reverence and adoration, which is certainly not limited to only singing praises to Him.
Worship can include giving (tithes, offerings, blessings), prayer and communion with Him, the way we speak, act and behave, the things we do in our daily lives, and the way we look after our bodies and love others.

Psalm 34:1, **"I will bless the Lord at all times; His praise shall be in my mouth."**
In this verse David exemplifies living a life of full-time worship. It is through worship that we experience a communion and fellowship with Christ that is continual (at all times).

John 4:24, **"God is Spirit, and those who worship Him must worship in spirit and truth."**

The Greek word for Spirit here is *"pneuma"* which translates as *"wind, breath, or air"* . God literally spoke everything into being with the very breath of His lungs through His spoken Word. So, worshiping in Spirit is an audible declaration of love with the breath in our lungs!

The Greek word for truth here is *"alethia"* which means *"what is true in any matter under consideration"* or *"what is true in things pertaining to God and the duties of man, moral and religious truth"*.

According to the Spirit-Filled Living NKJV Bible it *"denotes veracity, reality, sincerity, accuracy, integrity, truthfulness, dependability and proprietary."*

Worshipping in truth is coming before Him with a heart that is pure, and free from anything that is displeasing in His presence. We honour Him by living out and speaking out His truth through our actions and our heart posture.

Worship is warfare, it is powerful, and it is deep. Along with prayer, worship needs to be a non-negotiable element in your Christian walk.

Fasting

When we hunger and thirst for the Lord and respond in worship and prayer, it's like we are digging wells deep inside of us to carry anointing and to draw closer to Christ.
Fasting is another act of worship that helps us turn away from the fleshly desire to hunger and thirst for things of the world, and instead turn our focus on hungering and thirsting for the Word, the Spirit and the things of the Lord.

There are many benefits of fasting, including:
-increasing intimacy with God
-drawing us deeper into the things of the Spirit
-increasing clarity and helping us gain a heavenly perspective
-lifting our spirit and decreasing our fleshly desires
-helping us to build faith as we rely on Him to sustain us
-receiving revelation and breakthroughs
-it's good for your health (according to some health experts)

There are a few stand-out examples of fasting in the Bible. Moses, Esther and Jesus are a couple of these that we can look at.

Moses fasted and received the 10 commandments.
Exodus 24:28, **"So he was there with the LORD forty days and forty nights; he neither ate bread nor drank water. And He wrote on the tablets the words of the covenant, the Ten Commandments."**

Esther fasted for the safety of the Jews.
Esther 4:16, **"Go, gather all the Jews who are present in Shushan, and fast for me; neither eat nor drink for three days, night or day. My maids and I will fast likewise. And so I will go to the king, which is against the law; and if I perish, I perish!"**

Darius fasted for Daniel's safety in the lion's den.
Daniel 6:18, **"Now the king went to his palace and spent the night fasting; and no musicians were brought before him. Also his sleep went from him."**

Matthew 4:1-2, **"Then Jesus was led up by the Spirit into the wilderness to be tempted by the devil. And when He had fasted forty days and forty nights, afterward He was hungry."**
Jesus himself fasted and was led by the Spirit. This demonstrates how important it is for us to fast!

Fasting also allows us to truly humble ourselves before the Lord.
In Psalm 35:13 David says, **"I humbled myself with fasting".**

And in Ezra 8:21 it reads, **"then I proclaimed a fast there at the river of Ahava, that we might humble ourselves before our God, to seek from Him the right way for us and our little ones and all our possessions.".**

Fasting truly does humble us and allow God to move!

REFLECTION

A summary of what you learnt in this chapter.

REFLECTION

How does this challenge you personally?

REFLECTION

What is God saying to you personally?

APPLICATION

*How will you apply this practically in your life?
(your response to the last reflection question)*

PRAYER

Here is a space to journal a prayer or some prayer points based off your reflections and application to this chapter.

NAMES OF GOD

Another important aspect of having an intimate relationship with Jesus is that it helps us to BE more like Jesus, which should be our goal and desire.

-1 John 2:6, **"He who says he abides in Him ought himself also to walk just as He walked."**
-1 Corinthians 11:1, **"Imitate me, just as I also imitate Christ."**
-Ephesians 5:1, **"Therefore be imitators of God as dear children."**

We know that we become like those who we hang around with. The Bible is clear that our character and behaviour is to be like Jesus! In reality, it's who we are - the very DNA of Christ is inside of us through the Holy Spirit which helps us express the character and nature of Christ. However we need to KNOW Him, to be like Him.
When we understand who Christ is it helps us build a deeper, more intimate relationship with Him. Getting to know His character helps us to know and discern His voice and helps us build genuine relationship and trust.

Psalm 148:13, **"Let them praise the name of the Lord, For His name alone is exalted; His glory is above the earth and heaven."**

Who does the Bible say God is?
The Bible says God is Spirit (John 4:24), love (1 John 4:8,16), the way, the truth and the life (John 14:6), the Alpha and Omega, first and last, beginning and end (Revelation 22:13), the Rock, perfect, just, righteous and true (Deuteronomy 32:23). To name just a few!

An activity that I love to do is read through Psalm 139 and write down all the characteristics of God that are described in these verses. We can come up with so many words from just one Psalm! There are also specific names of God in the Bible that help us know Him better and this in turn helps us build a deeper relationship with Him. This is especially beneficial when it comes to discerning His voice as we grow in intimacy and communion with Him.

The following are key names of God and information about them found in the "Blue Letter Bible" (which is a great resource for studying the Bible and word study).

- **Yahweh: Lord, Jehovah**; "denoting the omnipotence of God, the absolute ruler, the Master. Yahweh is the promised name of God. This name of God which (by Jewish tradition) is too holy to voice, is actually spelled "YHWH" without vowels. While YHWH is first used in Genesis 2, God did not reveal Himself as YHWH until Exodus 3. In the Old Testament Yahweh occurs 6,519 times. This name is used more than any other name of God. Yahweh is first used in Genesis 2:4."
- **Jehovah Jireh**: The Lord Will Provide; "Jehovah-Jireh is a symbolic name given to Mount Moriah by Abraham to memorialize the intercession of God in the sacrifice of Isaac by providing a substitute for the imminent sacrifice of his son. In the Old Testament Jehovah-Jireh occurs only once in Genesis 22:14."
- **Jehovah Rapha**: The Lord That Heals; "Rapha (*râpâ'*) means "to restore", "to heal" or "to make healthful" in Hebrew. When the two words are combined - Jehovah Rapha - it can be translated as "Jehovah Who Heals." (cf. Jeremiah 30:17; Jeremiah 3:22; Isa 30:26; Isa 61:1; Psalm 103:3). Jehovah is the Great Physician who heals the physical and emotional needs of His people. In the Old Testament Jehovah-Rapha (The Lord that Heals) is used in Exodus 15:26."
- **El Shaddai:** All sufficient one, Lord God Almighty; "a God who freely gives nourishment and blessing, sustaining us. In the Old Testament El Shaddai occurs 7 times. El Shaddai is first used in Genesis 17:1."
- **El Elyon**: The Most High God; "expressing the extreme sovereignty and majesty of God and His highest pre-eminence. When the two words are combined - El Elyon - it can be translated as "the most exalted God."(Psalm 57:2). In the Old Testament El Elyon occurs 28 times. It occurs 19 times in Psalms. El Elyonis first used in Genesis 14:18."
- **Adonai: Lord, Master**; "Adonai is the verbal parallel to Yahweh and Jehovah. In the Old Testament Adonai occurs 434 times. There are heavy uses of Adonai in Isaiah (e.g., Adonai Jehovah). It occurs 200 times in Ezekiel alone and appears 11 times in Daniel Chapter 9. Adonai is first used in Genesis 15:2."
- **Jehovah Nissi**: The Lord My Banner, The Lord My Miracle; "Nes(nês), from which Nissi derived, means "banner" in Hebrew. In Exodus 17:15, Moses, recognizing that the Lord was Israel's banner under which they defeated the Amalekites, builds an altar named Jehovah-Nissi(the Lord our Banner). Nes is sometimes translated as a pole with an insignia attached. In battle opposing nations would fly their own flag on a pole at each of their respective front lines. This was to give their soldiers a feeling of hope and a focal point. This is what God is to us: a banner of encouragement to give us hope and a focal point. In the Old Testament Jehovah-Nissi occurs only once in Exodus 17:15"

- **Jehovah Raah:** The Lord My Shepherd; "Rô'ehfrom which Raah derived, means "shepherd" in Hebrew. A shepherd is one who feeds or leads his flock to pasture (Ezekiel 34:11-15). An extend translation of this word, rea', is "friend" or "companion." This indicates the intimacy God desires between Himself and His people. When the two words are combined - Jehovah Raah - it can be translated as "The Lord my Friend." In the Old Testament Jehovah-Raah (The Lord my Shepherd) is used in Psalm 23:1, Psalm 80:1, Genesis 48:15 and Genesis 49:24."
- **Jehovah Shammah:** The Lord Is There; "Jehovah Shammah is a symbolic name for the earthly Jerusalem. The name indicates that God has not abandoned Jerusalem, leaving it in ruins, but that there will be a restoration." He is there for us! "In the Old Testament Jehovah Shammah occurs only once in Ezekiel 48:35"
- **Jehovah Tsidkenu:** The Lord Our Righteousness; "*Tsedek (tseh'-dek)*, from which Tsidkenu derived, means "to be stiff," "to be straight," or "righteous" in Hebrew. In the Old Testament Jehovah Tsidkenu occurs twice, in Jeremiah 23:6 and 33:16."
- **Jehovah Mekoddishkem:** The Lord Who Sanctifies You, The Lord Who Makes You Holy; "Mekoddishkem derives from the Hebrew word *qâdash* meaning "sanctify," "holy," or "dedicate." Sanctification is the separation of an object or person to the dedication of the Holy. When the two words are combined - Jehovah Mekoddishkem - it can be translated as "The Lord who sets you apart." In the Old Testament Jehovah Mekoddishkem occurs 2 times, first in Exodus 31:13, then Leviticus 20:8."
- **El Olam**: The Everlasting God, The God of Eternity. The God of the Universe, The God of Ancient Days; "Olam derives from the root word *'lm'* (which means "eternity"). Olam literally means "forever," "eternity," or "everlasting". When the two words are combined - El Olam - it can be translated as "The Eternal God." El Olam is first used in Genesis 21:33, then Jeremiah 10:10 and Isaiah 26:4."
- **Elohim**: God, Judge, Creator; "Elohim is translated as "God." In the Old Testament Elohim occurs over 2000 times. Elohim is first used in Genesis 1:1."
- **Jehovah Shalom:** The Lord Is Peace; "Shalom is a derivative of *shâlêm* (which means "be complete" or "sound") Shalomis translated as "peace" or "absence from strife." In the Old Testament Jehovah-Shalom occurs only once in Judges 6:24."
- **Jehovah Sabaoth:** The Lord of Hosts, The Lord of Powers; "Sabaoth (se *bâ'ôt*) means "armies" or "hosts." Jehovah Sabaoth can be translated as "The Lord of Armies" (1Sa 1:3). This name denotes His universal sovereignty over every army, both spiritual and earthly. The Lord of Hosts is the king of all heaven and earth. (Psalm 24:9-10; Psalm 84:3; Isa 6:5). Jehovah and Elohim occur with Sabaoth over 285 times. It is most frequently used in Jeremiah and Isaiah. Jehovah Sabaoth is first used in 1Sam 1:3."

These are only some of the names of God! Having a greater knowledge of who God is increases our faith and authority because we can KNOW that we KNOW His truth! The truth of who He is unfolds as a profound revelation, progressively becoming an intimate truth within your heart.

REFLECTION

A summary of what you learnt in this chapter.

REFLECTION

How does this challenge you personally?

REFLECTION

What is God saying to you personally?

APPLICATION

How will you apply this practically in your life?
(your response to the last reflection question)

Here is a space to journal a prayer or some prayer points based off your reflections and application to this chapter.

REPENTANCE AS A LIFESTYLE

What is Repentance?

The Greek word for repent is *"Metanoia"* which means 'change of mind'. It involves turning away from sin and turning to God. It is the changing of heart, changing of self, changing of your current way of life. It means turning from one thing to another with remorse.

Joel 2:12-13, **""Now, therefore," says the LORD, "Turn to Me with all your heart, With fasting, with weeping, and with mourning." So rend your heart, and not your garments; Return to the LORD your God, For He is gracious and merciful, Slow to anger, and of great kindness; And He relents from doing harm."**

REND your heart; the Hebrew word for rend here is *"qāra"* which means to divide; break or tear, tear in pieces, tear away or out.

Interestingly, this word is usually used when speaking of clothing, however here emphasis is placed on rending the heart, not the clothing. This means that to really change your heart, you need to metaphorically tear out or tear away your old heart and allow God to make it new through His forgiveness and mercy as you repent.

True repentance means changing the heart, which in turn requires complete surrender; not just surrendering parts of you. Giving 99% of yourself to God isn't enough - this is an all-or-nothing decision we make in response to the 100% that God gives us. Jesus set that standard for us when He went to the cross so that we CAN give Him our all and repent and be made right with Christ.
So, to 'rend' our hearts we need to live a lifestyle of repentance and reflection.

Living a lifestyle of repentance is living a life surrendered to Christ and His ways, and living a lifestyle of reflection means taking time out with Christ to reflect on our character and our behaviours and adjust and repent accordingly.

2 Chronicles 7:14, **"if My people who are called by My name will humble themselves, and pray and seek My face, and turn from their wicked ways, then I will hear from heaven, and will forgive their sin and heal their land."**
Real repentance means changing your heart, and a complete change of heart requires more than a partial surrender.
I want to reiterate - giving God ninety-nine percent is not enough—you can't keep even one small part for yourself. This is an all-or-nothing decision.

Acts 3:19, **"Repent therefore and be converted, that your sins may be blotted out, so that times of refreshing may come from the presence of the Lord"**

Matthew 3:8, **"Prove by the way you live that you have repented of your sins and turned to God"** [NLT]

Proverbs 28:13, **"He who covers his sins will not prosper, But whoever confesses and forsakes them will have mercy"**

James 4:8, **"Draw near to God and He will draw near to you. Cleanse your hands, you sinners; and purify your hearts, you double-minded."**

1 John 1:9, **"If we confess our sins, He is faithful and just to forgive us our sins and to cleanse us from all unrighteousness."**

Revelation 3:19, **"As many as I love, I rebuke and chasten. Therefore be zealous and repent"**

2 Corinthians 7:10, **"For godly sorrow produces repentance leading to salvation, not to be regretted; but the sorrow of the world produces death"**

We need to repent, change our minds and then change our actions! God asks us to repent and we have to work with Him and obey Him! Always remember that this is a two-way relationship! We repent, then God cleanses and changes us on the inside, then we change our behaviours and way of life to align with the truth of what Jesus does through our repentant heart!
What an honour it is to partner with our Creator to live the life that He destined for us! And what a blessing it is that when we make a mistake or walk the wrong path, He is right here waiting for us to come to Him so that He can redirect us!

REFLECTION

A summary of what you learnt in this chapter.

REFLECTION

How does this challenge you personally?

REFLECTION

What is God saying to you personally?

APPLICATION

How will you apply this practically in your life?
(your response to the last reflection question)

Here is a space to journal a prayer or some prayer points based off your reflections and application to this chapter.

GLORY HOST

Leviticus 9:23-24, "**And Moses and Aaron went into the tabernacle of meeting, and came out and blessed the people. Then the glory of the Lord appeared to all the people, and fire came out from before the Lord and consumed the burnt offering and the fat on the altar. When all the people saw it, they shouted and fell on their faces.**"

Two key things from this scripture that always stand out to me are:
1. The need to be IN the glory to carry the glory.
2. The impact on others as a result of Moses and Aaron's relationship with God.

Let's look at the example of the woman who reached out to touch the cloak of Jesus (Luke 8:43-48). Jesus didn't teach the people that they could get well by touching his clothing; they simply OBSERVED the power of God working through him and responded out of desperation to what they could SEE was AVAILABLE!
People knew that Jesus continually carried that power because that's what they constantly witnessed! They could see the result of what it was like to work with God and being close to God, bringing Heaven to Earth. They then responded by reaching out, wanting to experience it for themselves.

Our intimacy with God is vital in order for other people to also experience Him!

We can also look at Acts 4:13:
"**Now when they saw the boldness of Peter and John, and perceived that they were uneducated and untrained men, they marvelled. And they realized that they had been with Jesus**".

Peter and John were recognised as ones who had been with Jesus simply by the way they carried themselves! This is the example for us to follow - To BE with Christ, and carry Christ; to BE in His glory, and CARRY His glory.

Smith Wigglesworth once said:
"It is not sufficient just to have a touch of God or to usually have a desire for God. There is only one thing that will meet the needs of the people today, and that is to be immersed in the life of God —God taking you and filling you with His Spirit, until you live right in God, and God lives in you, so that "whether you eat or drink, or whatever you do," it will all be for the glory of God (1 Corinthians 10:31)."

We need to be overflowing with His spirit, the way God desires it to be for us! Fully immersed in the life of God! This is what meets the needs of the people today. This is what fulfils us, and the only thing that satisfies us.

A quote from Bill Johnson that is great to challenge us is, *"Those who desire principles above presence, seek a kingdom without a king"* – we need to be constantly deciding to always be conscious of his presence; this is what increases impact!
It is this awareness that will manifest the principles of God's kingdom.

Intimacy with God, holiness and purity are keys to abiding in this place of being fully immersed in the life of God; of constantly being IN His glory.

Carrying His glory allows you to foster an atmosphere of "heaven on earth", partnering with Him, releasing Him, the person of peace and power, into the atmospheres, situations and environments that you walk into every day.

Habakkuk 2:14 reads, **"For the earth will be filled With the knowledge of the glory of the LORD, As the waters cover the sea."**

We have a responsibility to make known the glory of the Lord to the whole earth!

REFLECTION

A summary of what you learnt in this chapter.

REFLECTION

How does this challenge you personally?

REFLECTION

What is God saying to you personally?

APPLICATION

How will you apply this practically in your life?
(your response to the last reflection question)

PRAYER

Here is a space to journal a prayer or some prayer points based off your reflections and application to this chapter.

www.ingramcontent.com/pod-product-compliance
Lightning Source LLC
Chambersburg PA
CBHW061138010526
44107CB00069B/2982